Advance praise for *A REBELLION OF CARE*

"Where policy, programming, and posturing fall short, poetry delivers. Art is going to save us, and David Gate has given us the most gorgeous book of words that matter. I can't even pick my favorite poem, but these lines are from a contender: 'Though the system takes all it can / From our tired bodies . . . It will never, not ever, / Ransack our hallelujahs.' Come for the language, stay for the hope. What a gift. We need it right now."

—JEN HATMAKER,
New York Times bestselling author and host of the podcast For the Love

"This book invites you to be radicalized by tenderness. . . . A soulful refuge for both the cynic and the softy."

—LYNDSAY RUSH,
USA Today bestselling author of *A Bit Much*

"*A Rebellion of Care* is audacious, generous, and loaded with love. To read David's poetry is to be cracked wide open for the sake of beauty, wonder, and, most critically, each other. I haven't been this moved by a book in a long time."

—KENDRA ADACHI,
New York Times bestselling author of *The PLAN* and *The Lazy Genius Way*

"Good gracious, this book made me so glad to be alive in this beautiful tragedy of a world. *A Rebellion of Care* is a bracing pull-no-punches invitation to the disruption of joy, the tender work of healing, the demand of justice, and the stubborn ordinary holiness of being a person, despite all evidence to the contrary."

—SARAH BESSEY,
bestselling author of *Field Notes for the Wilderness*

A
REBELLION
OF CARE

A
REBELLION
OF CARE

POEMS & ESSAYS

DAVID GATE

 CONVERGENT | NEW YORK

Convergent

An imprint of Random House
A division of Penguin Random House LLC
1745 Broadway, New York, NY 10019
convergentbooks.com
penguinrandomhouse.com

LIBRARY OF CONGRESS CATALOGING-IN-PUBLICATION DATA
Names: Gate, David author
Title: A rebellion of care / by David Gate.
Description: First edition. | New York, NY: Convergent, 2025. |
Identifiers: LCCN 2025008061 (print) |
LCCN 2025008062 (ebook) | ISBN 9780593602171 hardcover |
ISBN 9780593602195 ebook
Subjects: LCGFT: Poetry | Essays
Classification: LCC PS3607.A78834 R43 2025 (print) |
LCC PS3607.A78834 (ebook) | DDC 818/.609—dc23/eng/20250319
LC record available at https://lccn.loc.gov/2025008061
LC ebook record available at https://lccn.loc.gov/2025008062

Printed in the United States of America on acid-free paper

3rd Printing

First Edition

BOOK TEAM: Production editor: Michelle Daniel • Managing
editor: Allison Fox • Production manager: Sarah Feightner • Copy
editor: Michael Burke • Proofreaders: Debbie Anderson, Jill Falzoi,
Andrea Gordon, Catherine Sangermano

The authorized representative in the EU for product safety
and compliance is Penguin Random House Ireland,
Morrison Chambers, 32 Nassau Street, Dublin D02 YH68,
Ireland. https://eu-contact.penguin.ie.

To my mother,

who taught me how to care and how to fight

CONTENTS

5. I POUR OUT THE CONTENTS OF MY NOTES APP IN AN ATTEMPT TO CREATE CONNECTION   85

6. THE TREE REMEMBERS WHAT THE AXE FORGETS   95

AN INTRODUCTION

Poetry is just the evidence of life.
If your life is burning well, poetry is just the ash.

—LEONARD COHEN

At the beginning of 2021, in a short fit of unmerited confidence, I began posting my poetry to Instagram with no great purpose or clear plan. I had decided to share a poem once a week for a year, regardless of how the pieces were received. A creative discipline. Zero expectations, just creating and sharing. Committing to such an intentional schedule of sharing your art is a commendable decision—but then you have to actually write the things.

Over that year, my poems scanned an array of recurring themes—friendship, stumbling faith, the rage & sorrow that comes with witnessing systemic racism and police violence, the dehumanizing effects of modern life, mental health, the physical body, and how to be kinder human beings in online spaces. My writing shifted between the physical, the metaphysical, and the supernatural, always colored by a political and spiritual undertone, even when those elements weren't explicit. It was a haphazard, scattergun, wing-it-every-week start to sharing online. Yet at the end of that year, as I stood back and examined these pieces as a body of work, one theme tied it all together: that the most important thing for us is to care for the world, ourselves, and each other. And more, to do so is a radical position, inherently undermining the status quo of twenty-first-century capitalism. I leaned in. I began to call it "A Rebellion of Care."

Though it may not feel like it, most of us already live radical lives—it is just not for anything we truly believe in. If you find it impossible to go to Target without spending $200 on stuff you had no intention of buying, you are already radicalized. Or if the only political options you can imagine are either old men in red ties or old men in blue ones. Or if the Amazon truck visits you every day. Or if you give 10 percent of your income to a church that spends only a fraction of that on helping the poor. Or if you bust your butt working as hard as you can at a career you don't enjoy, for a company that doesn't care about you, with the hope your body will last for more than five years of retirement. You are radicalized. These are extreme behaviors; we just call them normal.

I am interested in radicalizing us into a different kind of life—the kind of life you actually value most—a life of unrelenting care. I want to radicalize us into a life of self-acceptance that leads to other-acceptance. Into a life of nurturing what is unique about yourself so that you would nurture others in the same way. A determined life of tenderness toward bodies, spirits, minds, hearts—and the earth on which they live. A life of deep friendships that violate social orders of class, caste, individualism, and isolationism.

Many people have a dream of leaving society, going off-grid, leaving behind the digital age. There is a magnetic draw to a simpler life. Yet to create that life you have to rely on oil companies, Amazon, and tutorials from YouTube to even get started. That's not even mentioning the money required to begin and how you might go about acquiring those funds. True divestment from modern life is not a genuine possibility for most people. We remain complicit.

While you cannot break a system on your own, you can certainly weaken it. You can pull at its seams. Growing your own food, repairing your clothes, giving to mutual-aid funds all help achieve this. We have to build a new world while the old one decays—catching whoever we can and sparing as much of the earth as we are able. Not in an attempt to create some kind of impossible utopia, but for the objective good-ness of the task and the fate of the human soul.

A rebellion of care lies on the far side of cynicism. It is not before it—that is innocence. It is also not above it—that is naïveté. Instead, it is for those who know the patterns of cynicism because that is what the truth demands. It is for those who know the world is going to be cruel and that power inevitably corrupts all who possess it. A rebellion of care has been through a dark night of the soul.

If you probe the most cynical people, you will often find they are the most caring and empathetic. It is just that this world is so harsh, it feels like we have to encase ourselves in mistrust in order to survive. But we cannot stay in that shell indefinitely. It is a husk where souls wither and die. We have to break through the cynicism to exist in a second state of tenderness in the world. To be just as alive as when we were children.

That is not easily done, as very little in our world seems right these days. I know every generation thinks that, but we have more cause than most.

The rise of Christofascism, the corruption of our political parties by corporations and the ultra-rich donor class, the unfolding climate catastrophe, state-sponsored genocide, an oil-dependent food chain, AI devouring energy resources & creative jobs, monstrous rental costs, homeownership being a fantasy for most people, microplastics in everybody, greed under the veil of inflation while companies announce record profits.

The way our society is constructed is simply not good for us. It is not good for our bodies, nor our minds, nor our hearts. So what possible chance do our souls have?

I have voted "correctly" in every national and local election I was allowed to participate in. And still, things get worse.

I have prayed the right prayers with as much intensity as a human being can muster and given myself totally to religious practices. And still, things get worse.

I have protested at city halls and plazas, held signs and chanted under a punishing summer sun. And still, things get worse.

I have loved my family faithfully and fully and well. And still, things get worse.

Often I can feel myself inching closer to the lip of despair. Maybe you can too? But I'm not ready to give up just yet. I still want all of this life.

A hummingbird song. Blueberries, raspberries, gooseberries. Michelin stars and Taco Bell. Tattoos on my body where the skin will wrinkle as I age. I still want it all.

I want to listen to the rain while everyone else sleeps. I want to perfect a recipe. Make bad puns. Avoid the main story line with side quests. Sing three-part harmonies. Watch one more episode.

But I cannot positive-mental-attitude myself into a more equitable society.

I cannot keep practicing wellness in a hellscape.

I certainly can't stand opposed to the total power of corrupt corporations and a failing state on my lonesome.

Something has to change for all of us.

Something has to break.

As I am writing this, in October 2024, the city I live in—Asheville, North Carolina—has just been hit by Hurricane Helene. The floods, mudslides, and landslides have washed away entire neighborhoods. I am witnessing firsthand what a mass rebellion of care could look like. People are sharing and serving without hoarding or second-guessing themselves. Crisis brings focus. Our little fiefdoms mean nothing if our neighbor is dying. While the authorities may be here, doing what they are instructed to do, they are slow and inadequate. A trillion-dollar-a-year military is less effective than the organized, compassionate, and willing locals. Everything I see here tells me that a different way of living is not just possible; it is right under the surface of our society, ready to come alive.

We cannot rely on those in power to help us and we are going to have to make our own way. Of course good things can still be achieved by political and religious institutions, but we can't depend on them or place our hope in them to do what is necessary. They will never sacrifice themselves. We have to find other sources of power to help us. We have to bring that energy for each other.

We know what is true and we know what we must do.

The mystery of life is not "what is this all about?" The real mystery is "how do we forget?" The beginning & end of it all is that we must take care of each other. Anyone on their deathbed can tell you that & certainly every child feels it too. To say that "this life is beautiful" or that "love is the answer" is not in the least bit original, but it is the truth. I believe that truth still hums with possibility. And saying something true in a world awash with lies

is the first act of rebellion.

ONE

A REBELLION
OF CARE

A MANIFESTO FOR A REBELLION OF CARE

i.

Make art & music
because music & art
are love letters to the living
addressed to us all

Learn forgiveness
practice repentance
make reparations
carry no offense

In the accumulation of loss
retain an affinity for joy
& know that some truths
are only illuminated by tears

Listen to people's stories
like you are listening for a pulse
like you are in the cloud of transfiguration
rapt by the voice of heaven

If you see someone who is vulnerable
confused, lonely or lost
pick them up
& keep them going

Treat food & drink
& the tables you meet around
like the true religions they are
there is nothing more sacred

Temper the clamor for greatness
& become a student of goodness

in order to create
more beauty than toil

Turn from competition
let go of envy
bankrupt rivalry
& lift others up

No more grabbing
& taking & hoarding
instead we sway in the dance
of giving & receiving

Becoming something more co-op,
more kibbutz
more of that kumbaya shit

ii.

There are other ways to live
that need no flags or anthems
where we can all thrive
in the ceremony of nature

Tending to the fauna
cultivating the flora
keeping clean the air
keeping pure the water

Being equally fascinated
by stars & soil
stewarding the earth
in ways ancient & indigenous

Don't purchase your happiness
  —nurture it

iii.

Your best life
isn't to succeed
in every venture
while married to
the perfect partner
& moving in
an ideal body—
it is to love without fear

Always be totally yourself, but know
the most radical thing you can do—
    what will really change the world—
is to allow others to be *their* full selves
    in their complexity
    & their entirety
    & their absurdity

Dignity is the only thing that you can give
    that when given
    you will have more of
    than when you began

We contain multitudes
        therefore we exist
            in our own beings
                as community

Every law
every institution
every form of governance
is nothing more than an assent
Agreement is energy
& where two or three of us

are unified
there is the presence of God

So what do we owe each other?
    Nothing
    & yet, everything.

iv.

When you heal
    we all heal

So stay connected
to your own unique spirit
that you cannot be reduced
to an economic unit

Don't be so bound up
in your own problems
that you forget to be
either loving or grateful

Don't be so caught up
in existential despair
that you expedite the void
to our present moment

And if you feel yourself
shrinking away

like a fruit beyond
its moment of ripeness

pared back by daily grind
& algorithm

until all that is left
is the core of you

you are not diminishing
you are being left with nothing but

your sheer potential
the seed of something new

v.

Another way is possible

So I receive you as you are
because there is no love
without acceptance

I hold no claim on you
I have no shame to bear for you
all I have is yours

A rebellion of care
for earth
for each other
for your own tender frame.

THE GOOD WE CAN IMAGINE

This kale seed
I am planting in the soil
feels like throwing a pebble
at a panzer tank. It is
a tiny act of defiance
against the oil-dependent
insanity of our food chain
but still I must kneel
in the dirt and do what good
I can imagine
like forgiving someone who believes
they did nothing wrong
like a prayer for the dying

JOY IS AN ACT OF REBELLION

Joy is an act of rebellion
Against established order
That is why the angels
Brought their glad tidings
To the nightshift serfs
Rather than the boardroom suits
Because the joy of heaven—
Heralded to us—
Cannot be commoditized
Privatized or monetized
Though the system takes all it can
From our tired bodies
And stacks its weight
Upon our aching backs
It will never, not ever,
Ransack our hallelujahs

COMMIT TO THE BIT

If life is a comic tragedy
or a tragic comedy
it makes no difference at all
you still have to commit to the bit
you can't afford to half-ass it
whether you feel like the star
or a simple cameo
your task
is just the same
speak your lines
with voice of vigor
& with all your chest
like you believe
every word from your gut
because you are
the only one
who will ever get to play this part

DON'T GIVE UP ON YOURSELF

If there's a check engine light while you drive
& your card keeps getting declined
If you find yourself one bill from broke
& every plan just turns into smoke
Don't give up on yourself

Conjure up a cuss storm if you want
Curse the sky, the sun & the ground
Quit anything that makes you feel like shit
Toxic people, stupid habits, all of it
But don't give up on yourself

You can throw social media in the bin
You can rid yourself of politics or sin
Leave a church, leave a party, leave a job
Even a partner, if you must
Just don't give up on yourself

When all your hopes have journeyed to hell
And all your wishes are deep in a well
When all your prospects are grim
When all your chances are slim
Please don't give up on yourself

Good things take time
& good lives take the most
There *will* be good here for you
Just promise me one thing you'll do:
That you don't give up on yourself

WE ARE BORN TELLING THE TRUTH

We are born telling the truth
making cries
for our needs

But soon enough
we are taught
to stop speaking
unless it is urgent

That silence is a lie—
we shroud ourselves
in independence
to hide the helplessness

Yet the truth never changes—
I need you.

I WILL NOT NICHE MYSELF

I will not niche myself
because there is nothing more specific
than the entirety of a person.
I am not one thing
even if that thing is good
even if that thing is excellent
even if that thing is my livelihood
even if that thing is my calling
even if everyone loves that thing
even if people need it
instead, I will follow the muse
wherever she roams. I'm going to write
& paint & dance & scroll & sculpt.
I am not your poet, or your pastor
or your prophet. I am a steward
unto my spirit. I am a witness to my world.

WASTE YOUR LIFE

"You're gonna waste your life"
gosh, I hope so
writing poems
when I should be working
playing Super Mario Kart
with my ADHD kids
watching old movies
I know every word of
scrolling through memes
& laughing so hard
the people around me
demand to see them
praying for healing
that probably won't come
protesting unjust systems
I can barely imagine changing
yes, I want to waste my life
like a cocktail of tears & perfume
cracked open from alabaster

STARDUST

Remember you are dust
and to dust you shall return
however
it is stardust
so it's okay
to sparkle a little
before you go

STAY WEIRD

Make your corner of this planet
as weird as you want to
geek out in every way
your quirky heart desires
be a fan
be a stan
embrace obsession
value expression
remember that a doctor
is just a body nerd
and a rock star
is just a music dork
so there is no point hiding
all the ways you are unique
because every single one of us
is a gorgeous little freak

LESS PANIC, MORE DISCO!

Less panic, more disco!
Less cold, more play
Less guns, more roses
Less radio, more head
Less boy, more genius
Less daft, more punk
Less iron, more wine
Less flaming, more lips
Less vampire, more weekend
Less david, more bowie
However
More joy, less division

TERRAFORM

Write the world you wish to see
paint it or sing it or craft
take the thought of a new day
& let it become a path

Use whatever lies around you
the tools you have right now
& start the work of changing
making fertile fallow ground

It doesn't have to be a heaven
nor an idyll or an Eden
it just has to be a tomorrow
your soft heart can believe in

IT'S ALL A GIFT

The color palette when sunset
touches the cloud strata
the familiar patterns
of the moon cycle
that still, somehow
surprise us
the boredom
the ennui
the evenings of sorrow

I hope you know that
it's all a gift

so smoke the cigarillo
go to karaoke
add the fries
our time isn't slipping away
because we never held it
all we can hold
is grace & mystery
& the warmth of each other

TIME IS THE FACE IN THE MIRROR

i.

I thought by passing through the fire
I would be proved to be silver or gold
But there I found that I am glass
—an hourglass
pinched in the middle
watching the sand fall from one end to the other
there are more grains now in the lower half
than above. Life doesn't pass us by—
it passes through.

ii.

Every creak of my knees
Tick tock
Ever click of my jaw
Tick tock
My spirit is a candle
My body is a clock

iii.

Time is the face in the mirror
there is a child
in that face, an old man too,
we are all at once
past & present &
possibility

TWO

HUMAN BECOMING

Whether through entropy or evolution . . . nothing stays what it was.

My skin loosens as it thins
My nails soften as they grow
My eyes darken as they squint
My heart tightens as it slows
My mind forgets against its want
I am a human being. Always becoming.

Most of the physical changes we experience are involuntary, consequences of hormones and age. As our hairs gray and spines curve, we seek to assert control in various ways—diets, routines, exercises, potions & prayers—attempting to mold our bodies according to our will, until we realize the limits of our influence. The body will do what it was always meant to do. The rules cannot be unwritten.

There's a hint of madness in the futility of it all. Bodily standards and health advice are constantly shifting beneath our feet, with new rules, new diets, new strategies—each one promising transformation. We chase a fleeting version of ourselves, as though youth or perfection were something we could capture and hold steady in the palms of our well-moisturized hands. But it slips through our fingers every time. The whole enterprise—this endless project of self-improvement, this attempt to keep the body from what it knows how to do—leaves us exhausted, discouraged, and insecure.

If we want to move toward liberation, we must recognize the impermanence of our physical form. When we embrace the truth that life is fleeting, we have the potential to develop a more powerful sense of wholeness and sacredness, because we begin to grasp that our bodies are not negative or positive or even neutral. They simply are.

And then they are not.

We are born, we change, we die. Death is just one more transformation. In order to accept our own bodies, we have to first accept the impermanence of the whole absurd situation of being alive.

By relinquishing the manic urge to control and manipulate our bodies, we can redirect our focus and energy toward genuine self-care. We have to let go of this frantic desire to hold on to something that was never really ours to begin with so we can actually look after our bodies, in both health and appearance, liberated from the fear of aging and death.

This might mean listening to what our bodies need rather than forcing them into routines that exhaust or punish them. It might mean choosing rest over pushing through fatigue, eating foods that nourish rather than restrict, or moving our bodies in ways that bring joy rather than stress. By adopting practices like mindful movement, body acceptance, and compassionate self-talk, we can exist in ways that actually match our highest values of dignity and the importance of living life to the full.

The way we treat ourselves, of course, echoes in the way we treat others. If our internal lives are marked by managing, manipulating, and coping—then that's all our relationships will amount to. But if we can extend compassion to ourselves—if we can accept our bodies for what they are, for what they are becoming—then we can begin to offer that same care to the people around us. For who they are and who they are becoming. There's ancient wisdom in accepting our shared impermanence, and it is the foundation of a generous life.

TWERK OF ART

If you feel any joy whatsoever
that makes you wanna
shake your ass
you have to do it
you have to get up
& shake that thing
like the future
of the human race
depends on it
because I believe
it kinda does
it's of national importance
it's of eternal significance
it's an act of deliverance
so bounce it

SECRETIONS (NO SECRETS)

The saliva of our kisses
The sweat of our endeavor
The blood of our cycles
The colostrum for our children
The tears of disappointment
The snot from ugly weeping
The pus that comes with healing
The semen that creates

Why would we feel shame
                        for any of this life?

GOOD SKIN (A HAIKU)

Yes, I have good skin
it keeps the rain out and my
vital organs in

PUMICE

Tough at the heels
more scale than skin
I take the pumice stone
from the core of the earth
light & coarse
I put my elbow into it
to burnish the sole
until I recognize my own feet
as they were before the miles
how they felt as a child
softer now, I coat them in oil
anointing in reverse
every stony road I foundered on

BODY LANGUAGE

Whenever we divide our bodies
into what we like about them
and what we don't
we mutilate ourselves
you are not an inventory
of parts
in columns of pros
& cons
your body is more than gains
& losses
you are a whole being—
a poem
whose every word
makes meaning.

OLD LAYERS

Be at peace with the dust
you are creating
even as it shrouds
the mantelpieces & photo frames
& pictures of your younger years
when you were no more beautiful
than you are right now

NONETHELESS

Ask not if your body
is ready for the beach,
but if the beach
is ready for your body.
Be sure, reader,
it is not ready,
yet it will marvel
at your majesty
nonetheless.

SORRY (NOT SORRY)

Patiently, I watch
The cut upon my arm
Slowly close, then scab
Forming tender new skin
As I marvel at the magic of it
I remember
My healing does not depend
On an apology
That will never be given

HEATWAVE

The average human body is almost
ninety-nine degrees
so remember
at all times
you are hotter than a hot day
whether someone tells you or not
you are sultry
you're a scorcher
you're a sizzler
you're a veritable heatwave
and that is not opinion
it's science

WEAR WHATEVER

Wear whatever clothes
make you feel happy
(whatever happy means to you)
be comfortable
in your second skin
be prepared or smart
or chic or sexy
or simply warm
because the worst thing
you can possibly wear
is other people's expectations

THE WISDOM OF THE CHRONIC

The grinding of your teeth
The nights of insomnia
The knot within your gut
The skips of arrhythmia
Your body is a megaphone
For all that is inside of you
Imploring us to face
The symptoms of our trauma
So we can start the healing
Of the outer self & inner
Listening with compassion
To the wisdom of the chronic

LET ME GIVE YOU A MINUTE

There is a reason
why the doctor steps out of the room
while you peel off your clothes
only to re-enter
minutes later
and, promptly,
stare at your genitals.
Becoming naked
is more vulnerable
than being naked—
the process of revelation
is always the worst of it.

BEDFELLOWS

Grizzly bears get sleepy
and silverbacks too
lions are the kings
of the catnap
and tigers have little else to do
tiredness is not weakness
because strength & rest
are not strangers
they are bedfellows

THREE

FRIENDSHIP WILL SAVE US

For the last thirteen years I have lived four thousand miles away from my nearest blood relative who isn't one of my children. In that time, all our social and communal needs have been met by friends. Every single one.

Every meal cooked when we were sick. Every single babysitter. Every "need anything from the store?" text. A 2002 Honda Odyssey given because we were broke and had one too many children for a normal car. A small army of folks willing to fill a U-Haul. I know people move cities and countries all the time without forming any community whatsoever, but I don't know how. I don't think I would be strong enough for that.

There is a different kind of impact from receiving help from friends rather than family. It breaks the spell of our isolation. It is the feeling of being loved for who you are, not simply for your position in society or your family dynamic.

In a culture steeped in individualism and driven by the mechanisms of hyper-capitalism, the idea of friendship beyond the boundaries of family has taken on a certain urgency. We are told, repeatedly, that we must make it on our own, that independence is the goal, but the truth is we are lonelier for it. We scroll through our days, seeking connection in curated feeds, in half-formed conversations, convincing ourselves that this is enough. It isn't. Connection is made in the places we inhabit, with the people we meet there, in moments that don't ask to be posted or liked. These connections, fragile as they may seem, are what anchor us in a world intent on pulling us apart.

My life has been improved richly through internet friendships, and they have kept me alive through some dark times, but if all we have is online communities, then we are utterly beholden to the tech overlords. All they have to do is shut down our account or flood their own site with ads to the point of being unusable and we are left stranded from our online friends, totally alone.

Adulthood has always been like setting out to sea, but these days people who are entering adulthood are feeling totally adrift. There are fewer and fewer relational shores or harbors to settle in. But that doesn't mean we have to just give up, hold on tight, and try to ride the unpredictable waves of luck and privilege.

Many have noted that our society has evolved (devolved?) away from third spaces and community-based living, which for millennia has been the bedrock of neighborhoods and our support systems. Even the churches these days remain closed outside of Sunday worship. When everything is a business, and every local business is struggling, there is no margin to allow people to simply be together unless they are paying to do so at sufficient return for investors.

The act of nurturing genuine friendships and cultivating a spirit of communal reciprocity is the only way forward through huge societal upheaval and personal challenges. Though everything around us changes so often, the solidarity found in a web of caring friends establishes an essential sense of belonging. It provides a continually renewing sustenance and purpose.

Yet making friends in this age is no simple matter. It's not as if we were ever that good at it to begin with, but something about the pandemic sharpened the edges of our isolation, made us retreat further into ourselves and our enclaves. Now, with remote work and virtual everything, it's easy to feel like IRL connection is something we've forgotten how to do. People are busier, lonelier, more strung-out, and increasingly wary of each other. There is a thicker layer of fear to break through to make new friends. This sense of disconnection and trepidation is not unusual. It is everywhere.

The irony is, we are all feeling this same hunger for connection, even as we convince ourselves we're the ones who are left out. It's one of the few things we have in common now, this sullen desperation for some kind of community, some sense of belonging. And yet we remain apart, solitary, more comfortable in our isolation than we are ever likely to admit. But it doesn't have to be like this. There are ways back in, ways that aren't as impossible as they seem. Small steps: joining a local group, going to an event, sending a message to someone you haven't spoken to in years. It doesn't take much to break the spell of loneliness.

Because if we don't, if we allow ourselves to remain in this state of separation, we'll drive ourselves mad. We can't survive on family alone, much as we'd like to believe we can. Friendship is uniquely powerful because it is born from choice, not blood. I choose to be your friend & you choose to be mine. Familial love is the most natural thing on earth. Friendship, however, is supernatural.

A single family that is thriving is nothing more than one family thriving. But three friends looking after one another's needs is beloved community. And that is what will save us.

FRIENDSHIP WILL SAVE US

Friendship is what will save us
so fall deeply in love with your friends
date them, woo them, pursue them
mark your anniversaries
celebrate your victories
take care of their names
when they're not in the room
create a space for them
where all truths are tender
for intimacy doesn't have to be
reserved for romance
and crushes do not belong
only to lovers
so don't hide it
when you find
a bona fide ride-or-die

MUTUAL SANCTUARY

I place no demand that you bring
the very best version of yourself
to every occasion we meet
between us there is no contest
of composure or need to impress
you can show up with fraying strands
of cotton seams and DNA
jerry-rigged by the safety pins
of coffee and obstinance
we will both be present
in all our unraveling
make no attempt to get it together for me
we are together and that is all I need

GIVE FLOWERS

Give flowers to your friends
and poems to your people
make mixtapes and playlists
with songs you think they will love
call out the qualities
they cannot see in themselves
a single encouragement
can be enough nourishment
to sustain them through famine
and call them back to themselves
when they are lost and at sea
throw banquets of glee
for the heartiest of laughs
and ugliest of sobs
in a communion of saints
where the profound and profane
ring through the same air
share as much time as you can
before the finale arrives
for the quality of our friendships
is the quality of our lives

INTENTIONALITY

I am intentionally
and delicately
building an authentic
and safe community
of absolute fucking weirdos.

PRISMS

As we share the stories
of how we have been shattered

Light passes through the pieces
fractured into prisms

We see each other clearer
And more beautiful than if

We had never been broken at all

NEVER STOP SPAMMING THE TIMELINE

Never stop spamming the timeline
with all the things that you love
if you live in a beautiful place
show me
if you are in love
show me
if you ate something delicious
I wanna see
though I may skip through
the 207th baby pic
by God, still post them
your art, your music,
your kitchen designs
the books you have read
your poems that don't rhyme
fill this life with all you love
and share the joy with me

360°

The first thing
about knowing ourselves
is to realize
that we cannot
really be known
by our own eyes alone
we need to heed
what those close to us
perceive, because
we are too good
at the art of denial
too afraid of being
as naked as the lies
we tell ourselves

SO NO ONE TOLD YOU LIFE WAS GONNA BE THIS WAY

I want to pick you up from the airport at an ungodly hour & I want you to help me move my couch & I want to cancel plans & for you to not get upset & I want to look after your kids when you need a break & I want to open the good wine with you on a random Thursday & I want you to visit me in the hospital after hours & I want you to send memes when we both should be sleeping & I want to be waiting for you when you return from the vet, forlorn without your pet & I want you to side eye me when someone says something weird & I want to know what you need before you even have the words.

DROP YOUR GUARD

The hardest part of boxing,
For me, was not the punching
Or being punched
Or the dancing
But holding up my hands
For three minutes at a time.
Defending yourself
Constantly
Is exhausting.
Any relationship
Where you can drop your guard
is sacred.

I HOPE THIS FINDS YOU WELL

I type "lol"
even though I'm not laughing
I type "haha"
even though I didn't smile
I finish the line
with an exclamation mark
though there's nothing there
I need to exclaim
This is not to lie or fake it
I only want
to move gently
through our relationship
& for my words to feel safe
because I really do
want to find you well

CASPER

Maybe they're not ignoring me
Maybe it's just one of those days (or years)
Maybe they don't know how to respond
Maybe they're embarrassed
    it has been so long
Maybe they care so much
    it hurts to even speak
Maybe it's not about me at all

It's okay if you don't call me back
Because I have no desire to be
Another piece of personal admin
To feel guilty about
I want to be a shelter
Not a chore
A refuge for whenever
You need to make your way home

TO LAUGH WITH OLD FRIENDS

Our time drifts by
like a second glass of wine
in the hallowed safety
of history & trust
in the howling indignity
of belly cackles & snorts
a symphonic cacophony
of bountiful love
to the point where you can't breathe
to the point where I might pee
& through all manner of tears
our weary hearts revive
yes, to laugh with old friends
is to be truly alive.

IN MEMORIAM

I am so happy
to see you
at this funeral
because it's been
so long
since I saw you last
let's take a picture
together
in memoriam
sure, this feels
kinda wrong, but
soon enough
it will all be gone

LIKE EVERY SELFIE

Be kind about the names
Your friends give to their children
Praise their haircuts
Love their tattoos
It doesn't really matter
If that's what you would do
Like every selfie
All of them
Clap their songs
Cheer them on
You were born with a limitless
Supply of encouragements
Use every one of them
Don't wait for the eulogies
To speak out loud
That your friends are precious
And they make you feel proud

FOUR

THE IRREVOCABLE CONDITION

Perhaps home is not a place but simply an irrevocable condition.

—JAMES BALDWIN, *Giovanni's Room*

The family is under attack! But not from a queer agenda or communist ploy. It is under attack from the weight of expectation for it to fulfill every emotional and material necessity of human beings. It is an onslaught of patriarchal isolationism.

A husband, a wife, kids. One boy, one girl. Balanced, as all families are told they have to be. A monogamous romantic relationship that is meant to fulfill all our emotional needs. Children whom we use to justify every decision to isolate under the guise of protection—and whom we are relying on to look after us as we get older. And is the family home simply a place to fill with stuff? Until we need a storage unit?

We have to admit and face the difficulties of modern, homogenous home life and the aching we feel in the communal and spiritual deficit we have created by prioritizing marriage and children as the only forms of interpersonal fulfillment. By all means, get married and have kids. I did. But don't kid yourself that improving your family life will be the key to societal change.

Good families and good homes are not the goal. They are one solid foundation for children to blossom, and they are a playground for us all to learn commitment and forgiveness. But all that love and care isn't meant to form perfect picture postcards—it is meant to go forth.

Typically, we don't want it to go forth because people will find out the truth we work so hard to hide. We keep it all behind the IKEA curtains because, god forbid, people might actually see us for who we are. They'll notice how our love doesn't quite do the job, how our marriages are barely limping along, and how our parenting is more of an improv comedy sketch than a carefully curated lesson plan. Though this feels awful to reveal, it is actually a very healthy thing. The imperfect love my family has can fill some of the gaps in your family, and your imperfect love can fill some of the gaps in ours. But none of that can happen while we are all still pretending we have it all together.

To let those imperfections slip into the light is a necessary relief. And what you find when you let someone in on the chaos—when you admit that the love you give is far from perfect—is not a disaster zone but something else altogether: a place of real connection.

THE FONT

This kitchen sink, the font
of my home, where bread
pans soak & milk bottles
swill, where we wash paint pots
& brushes in the aftermath
of craft, where salad leaves
rinse to be rid of bugs & soil
where I clean the abrasions
of my working hands & all the blood
from the little cuts of constant use
in repetition & never-ending chore
I come to these sacred waters
daily to baptize the entirety of my holy life.

I TOLD THE PEONIES ABOUT YOU

I told the peonies about you
The orchids and dahlias too

They all said they were jealous
That I get to marvel at you

I told the peacocks and parrots
and they nodded in approval

Saying you are truly worthy
of the finest of plumes

I told the stars and they assured me
they had seen you out in your light

And that you were welcome to join them
to make bright the slate of night

I told God and she agreed
You are a wonder and an awe

And she lent me her words to tell you
just how beautiful you are

PALLBEARING

I try to savor each moment
like we're meant to
but moments are innumerable
& arrive relentless

> The hours I wish would hurry
> the years I wish would slow
> I can never get the record
> playing at the right speed

I want you to stay this age
making forts from cushions
chairs & old bedsheets
commandeering all the space

> And I also long to be done
> with all the clamber & chase
> I want to reclaim
> my living room

The noise you make
is a kind of music,
screamo, sure,
but you've made me hardcore

> The final piggyback ride
> before you got too big, neither of us
> remember. We had no idea
> it would be our last.

WHERE THE LIGHT IS GOOD

Let's go where the light is good
to capture this moment of love
between us. It makes bright
your eyes and strong my chin.
My right arm will hold us
steady, your smile will show us
happy. Can you send it to me
now? I will make it
my background. You will illuminate
every time I check my phone,
which is all the way
through the long damn day,
even when the light becomes
just a memory in the dark.

THE VARIABLE

There is little in life
more impressive than when
a person faces
the toxic patterns
of familial pain
and the recurring tremors
of trauma
then summons the courage
to address
every faltering father
& aura of ancestor
with the words
the past could not muster:
"The cycle ends with me"

DEPENDENTS

Dear houseplant*
I am very sorry
For watering† you
Too much
Or too little
I'm uncertain which

* child

† parenting

ON BOUNDARIES

I don't set boundaries
to make seeing you difficult
but to make knowing you
possible
they are not a threat
they are an invitation

THE CAT HAS GONE

The cat has been gone
Six days now
So I list the possibilities:

Lost
Wounded
Dead to the cold
Dead to a predator
Taken in by a more caring family

All possibilities
Equally horrifying

SWEAR JAR

I said "fuck"
in front of my kids
and my youngest
implored me to pay
into the swear jar
however, I only had a ten
so I had to get my money's worth

douchebag
dickhead
fuck
shit
fuck
shit
fuck
shit
balls

if the consequence for a crime
is only a fine
then it is only a crime
for the poor

CHERISH THESE YEARS

Telling me I must
"cherish these years"
I have with my children
has never once made me
"cherish these years"
but it does make me feel guilty
that I do not adequately
"cherish these years"
perhaps tell me instead
how you can help.

MICHELANGELO

How do you get a toddler
   to eat a broccoli floret?
Or a little kid to tie their shoes
   & leave the house on time?
Or teach a tween
   to be mindful of others?
Or coax a moody teenager
   to talk to you at all?
Creativity!
Being a parent
is the most creative calling on earth
so if you feel
like you have no energy or ideas
for anything else at all
it is because every single day
you are painting
a freakin' Sistine Chapel

PLAYING FAVORITES

Picking your favorite Bowie album
is like picking your favorite child—
it's an unfair & impossible task
yet I have an answer for both.

TELL ME AGAIN

When my child comes around
to tell me all about
the latest evolution
of some or other Pokémon
& I am too tired & grumpy
to care to listen
I try to remember that intimacy
is not all hugs & emotion
it is also the sharing of our selves
the who & what
& why of our selves
this makes them happy
so the choice is mine
whether I want to receive
the love they choose to give

CICADAS

If I had a button
That I could simply press
To take away your autism
I wouldn't press it
But if I could click my fingers
To understand how
You look upon the world
(As uniquely as you do)
I would click them so fast
& so often it would sound
Like an army of cicadas

WHO WEARS THE PANTS IN YOUR RELATIONSHIP?

Ideally,
neither of us.

LOVE IS AN OBSERVABLE PHENOMENON

Love is an observable phenomenon
like teardrops in a paper cup
& leaving people
better than you found them

Love cannot be parsed
into five languages—
your heart is a dialect
entirely of its own

You are a disco ball
& when the light hits you
a hundred rays
bejewel the room

Your name is a loanword from Avalon
I study your freckles
like Magi study the stars
your body is my scripture

I join the dots of your moles
like I am writing calligraphy
between the bars
of all our busyness

I love the urgency of your beauty
your steel constitution
the emergency of your desire
your tender energies

I kiss your neck
with the softness of a whisper
I chase your tongue—
listening as you speak

I don't want to wake you
so I shower in the dark
& close the door
as gentle as I can.

HOLY MOTHER

I see you
with your world in your arms
one life begets another

I see you
blood given
body stretched
and on occasion broken
but not like porcelain in pieces
like bread you're tearing open

I see you
with your heart outside your chest
still beating, swaddled at your breast

I see you
and this is why I must
worship God as Mother

PROTECTION RACKET

So you want to protect your wife?
I can applaud that
Protection is a form of care
But will you protect her dreams?
Support her career
Shield her free time
Guard her hobbies
Prioritize her mental health
Fortify her independence
Bolster her creativity
Ensure her agency
Defend her bodily autonomy
Even from yourself?
If not, then your *protection*
is just a racket

YOU GOT THIS

"You got this"
the influencer tells me
as I hide from my children
in the bathroom again
& consider my inadequacy
as both a parent
& a functional adult
so I scroll down

"You are enough"
doesn't quite cut it
when I am all out of time
out of money
out of patience
& the only abundance
in my house is screen time
so I keep scrolling

"You are a child of God"
I read upon the throne
of my toilet seat
& I wonder to myself
if he hides in the bathroom sometimes too?

TELL ME ABOUT YOUR PERSON

Tell me about your person
   the one that you lost
   the one that you miss

Tell me about their quirks
   their habits & their tics

Tell me about their loves
   their magic & their bliss

You don't have to forget
   or paper the cracks

Because grief & gratitude
   are parallel tracks

For a train that doesn't stop

So if your person is a part of you still
   tell me their truth

I want to know them
   because I want to know you

I STILL GET TO BE YOURS

On the days when there is not
enough coffee in the pot
   I still get to be yours

When our griefs are overlapping
like they're a herringbone pattern
   I still get to be yours

As the bags beneath our eyes
grow wrinkles at their sides
   I still get to be yours

When the kids we made are shouting
When the dogs we bought are barking
When the baby goats are dying
When the friend we lost is lying
When the country is on fire
Inflation getting higher
And our troubles all are rhyming
   I still get to be yours

FIVE

I POUR OUT THE CONTENTS OF MY NOTES APP IN AN ATTEMPT TO CREATE CONNECTION

A

Accretion
A commotion
A culture of consumption is a culture of destruction
Add to cart
Advocate for your own orgasms
Aggressive Normality
A hall of mirrors
All luck is rotten for someone
All pleasure is guilty pleasure if you have enough religious trauma
All that I know came after a lifetime of not knowing at all
All theology is fan theory
A menace to myself
A million cars idling
A reflection of a reflection
Asking questions increases user engagement
A weighted blanket
A withered mulberry bush

B

Back on my bullshit (as if I ever got off)
Behind a velvet curtain or a chiffon veil
Being late is not a moral failure
Be very careful today because I am taking everything personally
Boss battles
Brains can be bastards
Bread that doesn't mold
Burnout epidemic

C

Carnations & darnations. I romanticize my life.
Celebrate everything you can
Change is never on the ballot

Chaos where there should be order
Cliques are good actually
Comment Section Blues
Compliance but let's brand it as "Character"
Concertina
Contraband

D

De-escalation is an essential skill
Deflating the inflatable Santa
Dis-content creators
Do Not Resuscitate
Don't abbreviate yourself for me
Don't forget to like & subscribe
Doomscroll the gallery of human suffering

E

Envy is the thorn prick from a rose
Eventually there will be a year where I won't see its winter
Every gas station is our canvas. Go paint.
Every tear is a memory
Everything costs so much, it's almost worthless
Everything the light touches

F

Faith is a shattered jar
Filters can't hide exhaustion if you are tired in your very soul
Flesh is only borrowed dust
Full like a child's pocket

G

Genesis is my favorite creation myth
Get good at goodbyes. You will not regret it.

GGs is a way of life
Ghost notes
God made me in his image and I returned the favor
Gonzo Theology

H

Headphone bleed
"He's one shot" is my favorite lie
Hope is always on the brink
Hunched over a stool at an upright, as the last piano hit rings into
    silence
Hydrate or Die is not hyperbole

I

I am not alone if I'm able to recall what I mean to you
I don't feel like leaving anymore
I don't know any of the special moves, I'm just mashing buttons
I expected more from a poet
I know why they call it "a nervous system"
In shards
In the early sleep where the first dreams die
I resent having to drive everywhere
I try to make the last bite the best
It's not chaos if you know what you want
It's not doomscrolling if the doom is reality
I will never know what anyone thinks of me
I would swap all the hustle in the world for one drop of true patience

J

Janice was a better person than all the FRIENDS
Jesus said don't worry, not don't care
Joy isn't always a choice, but when it is, choose it
Judgment is the enemy of kindness

K

Knee. Jerk. Reaction.

L

Laminate me, o god
Let strangers see you cry
Let's just say you love me
Life is a buddy comedy where you die at the end
"Lived experience" is a tautology
Living from one beverage to the next
Love wins, but first it loses

M

Make me incomplete, by which I mean: keep the hunger alive
Mid-frequencies
Minimalism is the hatred of children
Mistakes I don't regret
Mo money, mo problems (they are just the problems you want to
     have)
My kid calls him "Jesus Crisis"

N

Nobody needs a second job, they need justice
Not every contradiction is a hypocrisy
Not fully known, like magnetism or mushrooms
Nothing hurts like realizing your high school bully became a better
     person
Nothing personal
No trees left to burn
No tv static, just lag

O

Often you cannot hold the truth in a way that doesn't hurt
Only missing white girls make the news
Only the living have stories, songs, and scars
Order where there should be chaos
Our needs do not become valid only when we become productive

P

Pecking cheeks in passing
Pick your painkiller
Pidgin
Podgy
Poems that are slogans
Poems that are soundbites
Police violence is just the cost of doing business
Pretending to care is often a form of caring
Pumpkin spice is not a personality, but neither is hating it

Q

Queering the multi-verse

R

Ramshackle
Reading everything in Dark Mode
Red Hat is an anagram of hatred
Run-of-the-mill dystopias

S

Sacrilege
Self-made trillionaire
Sob stories

Some rejections are mercies
Spitting scripture like the Devil in the wilderness
Subterranean Homesick Influencer

T

Tantamount to love
The beauty of an ugly cry
The child surpasses the father
The Devil's Lyre
The gods we make for ourselves
The hard part isn't getting free, it's staying free
The lynching tree, a southern cross
The news is never all bad, only what they show
The racists will be fine. That's the tragedy of it
There are some deaths that don't kill you
There is no such thing as ethical consumption
The smell before it rains
The span of life between suffering & boredom
The universe was born in love
They will go as far as we will let them
Time constraints
To enjoy the magic you have to suspend your disbelief
Too good not to share
TV made us docile, scrolling makes us paranoid

U

Undulation
Unreliable narrators
Until we are all free
Untitled playlists

V

Victims of time & money

W

Waist Management
"Waste not, want not" I did not waste, yet I still wanted
We all live overseas
We are ronin, not ruled by master, but by code
Wedlock? Gross.
We go wherever we feel safe
We've either all seen God or none of us have
Whatever gets you through
Whatever you can name, no longer controls you
When life gives you demons, make demonade
When people ask me about trauma, I tell them about you
When we love we feel our most immortal
Whiskey in the milk
Whiteness is theft
Why can't you say the words I want to hear?
Wiseacre
Workaday
World-forming

X

Xanax side effects include dizziness, changes in sex drive, &
    loquaciousness

Y

You are somebody else's heretic
You can't have momentum—you are momentum
"Youth" is dying at a pace you can't perceive

SIX

THE TREE REMEMBERS
WHAT THE AXE FORGETS

The axe forgets; the tree remembers.

—an African proverb

I remember the day we sat down as a church staff, and we were told that we were going to start measuring everything. Not just the attendance numbers for Sunday services, but every event, every ministry. A metric for this, a percentage for that. The volunteers would be numbers, the members would be numbers, and of course, the unsaved would be entered into a database. They didn't phrase it that way, of course, but it was clear.

I dissented and paraphrased Goodhart's law, which says that "when a measure becomes a target, it loses its effectiveness as a measure." None of the leaders knew what I was talking about. I had the sinking feeling that we were becoming rats in a maze, learning how to get the cheese, learning how to manipulate the numbers instead of caring about the actual names and lives attached to them.

It's a strange thing, living in a system that asks you to quantify the unquantifiable. To put a number on faith, on kindness, on the intangible web of human connection. All of us can read the right books, develop all the right principles—sustainability, social justice, compassion— and still find ourselves trapped in a world that rewards us for gaming the system, for making the right gestures while real progress slips further out of reach.

There is something grotesque about a system that claims to elevate humanity while quietly grinding us down, turning every act of rebellion into another act of compliance. The system persists not because it is strong, but because it convinces us that it's the only way. Capitalism, consumerism, neoliberalism—whatever name you give it—the effect is the same. You start to believe you're moving forward, but it's a treadmill, and you're just getting tired.

And now the mantra is that we should take care of ourselves. Self-care, as if the problem is just us. Vitamins, water bottles with inspirational quotes, step counters on our wrists. Trying to become so busy monitoring our own wellness that we forget the world is on fire. We meditate, we do yoga, we drink our green juices and try to convince ourselves that we have a modicum of control. These things are a way to cope with the fact that we can't actually stop the system from slowly suffocating us. It is an insistence on individual well-being while the collective well-being crumbles around us. But we cannot keep performing wellness in a hellscape.

Most empires fall when they are devoured by another, when a greater force overcomes them. But what is unique about capitalism is that it teaches us to devour each other. It feeds on us until there is nothing left to consume. The system persists by pitting us against one another, convincing us that our worth is tied to our output, that scarcity is inevitable, and that success requires competition rather than collaboration. It thrives as long as we keep playing by its rules, blind to the damage it inflicts on us and the planet. And it will only end when there is nothing left—when we've devoured ourselves, leaving nothing behind but the charred remnants.

I feel stuck in a rhythm that is not my own, driven by a system that thrives on perpetual motion and constant productivity. Even something as simple as going for a walk to clear my head feels like it needs a destination, a purpose. Why can't I just walk? Why must everything be productive, even my relaxation? The problem is terminal.

Sometimes I wonder if we have forgotten who we are. I look at the charismatic leaders, the politicians, the activists who once promised a better world, and I wonder if they remember. Or if, like so many before them, they've been swallowed by the very system they swore to dismantle. And then I wonder if it's happening to me too. If it already has. I've seen people I love transformed into something they never wanted to be—cogs in a machine they once railed against. And I wonder in what ways I have stopped railing and started accepting.

The axe forgets itself. But the tree remembers. I remember the sharp sting of each blow, each small compromise that felt like nothing at the time but became everything. And now I am here, watching the trees fall, watching the world we hoped for slip further away. But I also know that remembering is a kind of resistance. There is still hope in the act of remembering, hope that we won't become the axe, that we won't lose ourselves completely to a system that devours.

Apathy is the first enemy. It is the soul killer, dulling our senses until we stop caring, until we stop trying. But in a world like this, generating enough empathy to fight back the apathy can feel like an impossible task.

Sometimes the only antidote to apathy is anger.

THE PROBLEM OF HAPPINESS

People say "money doesn't make you happy"
but we know that is nonsense
it definitely makes you happy
every pay rise
tax rebate
birthday card with cash
made me happy
it made me happy
until it didn't
the problem
is not the money
it's the happiness
it glitters
but doesn't stick
that is why I don't seek happiness
I seek joy
because joy is not the outcome of getting everything you desire
it is knowing that *to desire at all*
is to be totally alive

TODAY IS THE FOURTH OF JULY

Today is the Fourth of July and half those stripes & all those stars are white. The rest is blood and sky. Today is the Fourth of July and if America has any greatness it was built upon the labor of slaves, the toil of the underclass and the continually underpaid & unpaid work of women. The founding slaveholders had some big ideas but ideas can't be kept in shackles; they belong to everyone. Today is the Fourth of July and the only real freedom is the freedom to consume and Joey Chestnut wears the crown. Today is the Fourth of July and there are two Americas: one for Tamir Rice & another for Kyle Rittenhouse. Or perhaps the latter requires the former and there is just one America. Today is the Fourth of July and that flag fitfully blows, of snow & ocean & wilting roses, it half conceals and half discloses.

IT TAKES A VILLAGE

It takes a village
but there are no villages out here
only suburbs
& endless city
only ghost towns
where the bonfires burn low
& the barns are no longer raisin'
& the rusted water towers lean.
Where are we to go?
There is no "where" I can see
I can only see "how"—
Will you be my village?

EMAIL UNTO OTHERS

Email unto others
as you would have them
email unto you
(rarely
& only delightful things)

IF YOUR DREAM ONLY INCLUDES YOU, IT'S TOO SMALL
(After Ava DuVernay)

An eagle in flight is such
a magnificent sight. No doubt

about that. Nothing seems as free.
But I don't want to be an eagle.

I want to be a starling. To traverse
the skies in stunning murmuration

I want you & I & all our people
to swoop & soar. Together we can

grace the sky in concert & dance
None are free until all are free.*

I don't dream of the grandeur of flight—
I dream of a world without cages.

---

* "None are free until all are free" is an approximation of a quote from Emma Lazarus.

LIVING IS ALWAYS THIS INSTANT

From the exit of the highway
I peek at the Blue Ridge mountains scenery
Obscured by all the gas signs
Those 30-foot monstrosities
Selling petrol for SUVs
Selling Slim Jims and blue Powerade
Why sell anything edible?
You'll only vomit anyway
Living is always this instant

From the hotel room downtown
I can walk to all the upscale bars
Turning up their microphones
To drown out the humming of idle cars
Selling domestics and one IPA
Selling barely alcoholic cocktails
Who gives a damn about value
On the backside of the working day
Living is always this instant

From the police line by the stadium
The civic tanks meet protest
A diverse force for the cameras
While the people live in unrest
Selling bluelines to the gullible
Stealing black flags from guerrillas
Policing nothing but the property
Of the city's major donors
Living is always this instant

From the talk show on the radio
To pimped out televisions
The wagging tongues and tidy lips

Of the puffed-up politicians
Selling promises of this and that
Selling hatred by the truckload
Claiming they can build the future
As if they didn't shit the bedroom
Living is always this instant

IN THE NAME OF CONVENIENCE

We drive thru the coffee shop
the pharmacy & the bank
because no conversation
is convenient

We buy furniture from IKEA
made of chipboard
destined for a landfill
because no creation
is convenient

We buy new clothes
instead of sewing up seams
we like our fashions fast
because no craft
is convenient

We make playlists
& find podcasts
to get our spiritual fixes
because no church
is convenient

We sacrifice so much for our convenience
Yet everything remains
Almost impossible

TRUST FALLS ARE EASY

Trust falls are easy
because there are very few people
in life who want to see you
break your back.

Of course your boss is going to catch you.
They don't want to be sued.
But will they give you healthcare?
Maternal leave for newborns?
Parental leave for old-borns?
Dignity? Basic human dignity?

It's not your back they are willing to break:
It's your spirit.

IMPOTENCE

I want to hug my children tonight because I love them and not because I am relieved they were not killed in this week's mass school shooting. I want to look at them with tear-filled eyes of tenderness for their own beautiful beings and not because I know this country could rip them from me at any moment. I want my little ones to see my love stemming from them alone and not because their father is haunted by the news; the news that doesn't change; the news we could become.

WORLD SERIES

Across the pond
we have all the same video games
and we despair
in all the same kind of ways
and we have our fair share
of mental illness

We take the same meds
Make the same music
Watch the same movies
Have all the same kind of fun
So what is the only difference?

By Jove, my Yankee cousin
It's the motherfuckin' guns

I SUPPORT THE TROOPS

By which I mean I hate war
And every pretense
Generals and politicians
Coax the poorest kids
Out of their hometowns
To kill the indigenous
Of foreign lands
To create new markets
Before the mothers
Watch their children
Buried under a flag
& six foot of stolen soil
With more guns in their salute
Than years on the planet

I would reassign every prodigal dollar
We lavish on murder machines
Into medical care
& mental health provision
For every Vet
In aeternum
And turn each bullet into a rivet
To build houses
& fix the bridges
Of our crumbling infrastructure
That so many of those soldiers
Are made to sleep under
So make no mistake, I support the troops.

AVOCADO TOAST

It's a fucking slice of fruit
On a fucking piece of bread
Not a lobster tail
At the fucking Ritz-Carlton
What the fuck do you want us to eat?
Your fucking crumbs?

INSATIABLE

The most difficult part
of helping the poor
is not calling
for the hungry
to be fed
but for the wealthy
to be content

SHEEP & GOATS

There are those
Who struggle
To earn

And those
Who struggle
To share

I know which I'd rather be
On the day of judgment

THIS IS NOT A RACE

This is not a race
and you are not a straggler
because what you do
& who you date
& where you live
is not a competition
all the markers
given to you
for the story of your life
don't actually exist

but you do—
    your vibrant being
        & precious days

the time is yours
so stroll through this life
no faster than
the pace of your pleasure

OPTIMISTIC

I'm reaching for notes
I can't really hit
I'm wearing favorite clothes
That no longer quite fit
I'm planting up trees
For fruit I won't eat
I'm dancing too awkwardly
Just a touch off the beat
I'm raising up kids
On a planet that's warming
I'm still eating cheese
With a cholesterol warning
This is the way I'm choosing to live
Alive with no shame and no fucks to give

HOPE IS NOCTURNAL

Hope is nocturnal
It comes from the light
But does not belong there
Preferring the darkness
To sharp brightness
For it has no purpose
Where hearts will believe
Happily what they see
So it makes a home
In the deep shadows
Where it waits to be found
By those who need it most.

SEVEN

SOFT FASCINATION

I grew up in London so I am familiar with gray skies and the constant threat of rain. But even an English upbringing did not prepare me for living for three years in Belfast, Northern Ireland, where it rains three hundred–plus days a year—a city surrounded by hills of deep green and cloaked in gray.

In 2011, I moved to Florida where it is forever summer. Where you wear shorts on Christmas Day. Where SPF saved me daily from lobstering my daisy white skin. If you have children in Florida, it is damn near impossible to survive without a pool. We didn't have a pool. Perhaps the thing I found strangest about living in North Florida is that there is no autumn or fall. The trees shed their leaves whenever they feel like it. Whenever they get dry or a bit bored. The gutters need clearing all year round.

My experiences in mono-climate environments have taught me that I need the seasons. I have a near spiritual need to witness the cycles of life. I need snow and I need spring. I need to see things bloom and I need to see them die. And as I get older, I even appreciate the winter more. It is less of a sensual assault than the summer.

Octavia Butler says "God is change." I feel the truth in that as I experience the seasons. While it is hard to watch the garden wither in the late autumn, I am glad to see the weeds die. I tire of digging up pokeweed roots and trimming the ragweed. Everything grows in the North Carolina summer; not all of it is good. And though the winter brings us less to harvest, it is easier on my body. Spring is a joy. Fall is a panorama of claret & gold.

I used to be the cliché that would say "I always double the garlic in a recipe." No recipe was ever garlicky enough for my tastes. That was until we grew our own. The garlic we grow is ten times more potent than what we bought in the store. The yolks in the eggs from our chickens are orange. You could never mistake them for yellow. Everything we make is richer and stronger and better. The world I was given is a specter of what it should be.

I am still deeply romantic for the great cities of the world, but a tangible connection to the living seasons is essential for my mental health and my soul. I understand why some people would rather live in a park than a shelter.

If the physical world is the transfer of energy, then the spiritual world is the transfer of attention. To observe and participate in nature is to tend to your mind, body, and soul.

Appreciating the natural world needs to be more than the occasional sunset pic. And caring for it has to be more than a paper straw.

To live with the names of native trees, birds, and plants unknown to you—you may as well be passing through a foreign country with no language at all. There is a peace in knowing the name of the oak that shades your backyard, or the cardinal that flits between the branches. This knowledge reminds us that we're a part of a larger order—a delicate ecosystem that exists whether you notice it or not. To know the name of a thing is the first step toward caring for it, for we cannot protect what remains anonymous to us.

Despite our ignorance, looking after these things is not grand or dramatic—it's a matter of noticing, of joining the rhythms already in motion. When you learn the life cycle of a butterfly or understand the migratory path of the birds that rest on your windowsill, the world becomes less about your immediate crises and more about the totality of life that lives beyond our anxieties. The small acts of nurture, whether it's planting native species or leaving space for wildflowers to flourish, create a reciprocal relationship between you and the land. You grow from being simply a resident in passing to the seat of custodian.

We talk a lot about being "centered" or "grounded." Yet there is nothing more grounding and humbling than having your knees in the soil with a seed and a dream. Then having your dream eaten by a jackrabbit. And then picking up your trowel and dreaming once again. It is desperately human.

SOFT FASCINATION

Alive, I am walking through old trees
that feel as healing as balm or prayer
I catch aromas of heather & pine
slowing the pulse of thought & progress

The pendulum within slows its ceaseless swing
between the overwhelm of task & labor
& the underwhelm of chronic boredom
I must pay attention to what I cannot possess

I glimpse the morning moon in the clearing
of bright bluebells and stop, flower-rapt
I am awake in a forest of being—
changing nothing here but where I tread

I name the sights, I name the smells
I name the sounds of nightingales,
warblers, the wind in the leaves,
a distant, young child & the brook

I am only moving where my body goes
no automobiles, no aeroplanes
that throw me wherever I am told
I have to be

It seems to me that I could become rooted here
my feet sinking into the earth to belong
but also, that I could leave
to soar with the goshawks

So it is
to be human

Receiving the world in soft fascination
to rediscover ourselves;
our nature, our supernature,
& the spirit that animates our fragile existence

EAT THE SEASONS

In spring, we pluck the tender greens
asparagus spears & artichokes
everything the frost couldn't steal
is a foretaste of what is to come
the earth moves to bud & bloom
    in the first days of the coming light
    we eat the seasons while they're ripe

In summer, we pick the succulent fruits
peaches & cherries & peppers
all the berries from the bush
for they are here for little longer
than a cycle of the moon
    on the longest day & shortest night
    we eat the seasons while they're ripe

(It must be said—eating a tomato out of season is a sin against nature
    and in defiance of God)

In autumn, we don't miss a beet
or pear or persimmon or pumpkin
this is the time of harvest
to pickle & preserve
to help get us through the cold
    the earth has enough if we're willing to learn
    we eat the seasons in their turn

In winter, we pick the hardy greens
lacinato kale & kohlrabi
brussels for the holy days
when we are most grateful
for everything we are given
    on the shortest day & longest night
    we eat the seasons while they're ripe

A LESSENING

I do not plan to start anew
in January
that is for spring
this is the night
in the dead of winter
where I pare back excess
to reach the bones of my life
so when I am reborn
I am reborn as only
my most essential nature

JANUARY

I don't want to leave the warmth
of the bed to get into the shower
I don't want to leave the warmth
of the shower for the icy bathroom tiles
Pretty snow
      becomes shitty sludge
It's the slowest month
      after the quickest year
Looking forward (hope)
Looking forward (anxiety)
Picking up everything
      I put off
Asking the big questions
Not liking the big answers
Stew and soup and broth
Everything cooked
      in the same old pot

YOU MUST BELIEVE IN SPRING

You must believe in spring
As the pine mulch
Keeps the warmth
In the earth
Back and forth
Carbon, diamond, coal
Cloud, rain, thirst
Everything is always returning
Like a hero from battle
Back to the beginning
Even the evergreens
Die in their time
So you must believe in spring

NOW AND NOT YET

Caught between the seasons
    of winter and spring
is that snowflakes or blossoms
    that float on the wind?
morning cold & evening warm
    outfit plans are pure folly
newness arrives with a chill
    like my favorite kind of melancholy
a strange revelation
    to find in meditation—
it is colder on the days
    when the sky is sheer blue.

DOES A TREE DESERVE TO GROW?

Does a bird deserve to fly?
Or a fish deserve to swim?
That's how ridiculous we sound
Whenever we ask
"Do I deserve to be loved?"
You were created for love,
It's the reason you are here—
To give love & receive it.
It is your purpose.
"Deserve" doesn't come into it.

CURSE THESE MINUTES

Curse these minutes
and damn these clocks

to think of life in units
of hours & minutes

is like talking about a newborn
as atoms & cells

it tells you nothing
of what it is

give me the days
of dawns & dusks

give me the months
of cycles & moons

give me the years
of summers & springs

of winters & falls
of solstice & equinox

but curse these minutes
and damn these clocks

CLEMENCY

We need a new word
for enjoying the unseasonal
clement weather while also
feeling the creeping despair
of climate catastrophe.
Perhaps the Finnish
already have a word?
Others realize these things
long before the land of the free.
While we are just staring
at the crest of a volcano
pretending the ending
isn't written in lava.

EMBEDDED

I came across a metal sign
hung on a tree
that over time
became embedded
into the wood
bark engulfed
the foreign notice
until what was alien & what was natural
were indistinct
like how the grief we swallow
in sips & gulps
absorbs into our being
it fails to catch the eye
of a passerby
but for those who stop
and stare, they will see
something that wasn't always there

INDOORSY

Spend a sunny day
indoors, if you want
and feel no shame
for reading a book
or playing games
or napping in your bed
all of this—is life as well
and you are as wild
as anything out there

REWILDING

I don't mow anymore
because of the gas & the noise
& the heat & the death
to the pollinators & their habitats
& because I care less now
about what neighbors think
but so much more
for our earth & her lifeforms
& her rugged greenery
& what we cannot let die
on our watch. I won't be
mowing Eden to inches
to feel like I am a god.

MADE OF STONE

A hot stone
   to steam the sauna
a cold stone
   to mill the flour
a rough stone
   to smith the sword
a smooth stone
   to skim the lake
There is no such thing as a wasted life

LEGACY

Take my ashes and scatter
them at some allotment
or vegetable plot
    I don't want to be buried
    in a graveyard
    forgotten
Instead it would be an honor
to become compost for a squash
destined to splatter
a toddler face
and bib
and high chair
    and hopefully he eats enough
To fill his small belly
    so he may enter
    a long night of slumber
Then his mother may know
peace of her own
    That would be
    some elegy

WINTER'S INSISTENCE

The leaves have fallen into the earth
alongside my romantic notions
of changing seasons
just the starkness remains to teach me

But I don't want hard lessons
I want leaves
beauty with ease
not winter's insistence
that I learn to grow
every single year
to see the world anew

& yet, somehow,
I always do.

EIGHT

I MUST ALSO
FEEL IT AS A MAN

I have had to overcome a number of personal shortcomings on the journey toward emotional health. Firstly, I am a cis man and there are only two emotions we are permitted to express in our culture: we can be angry, and we can be horny. That is all. I also had a Christian upbringing so the anger had to be righteous and the horniness had to be wed. To add to that cocktail, I grew up lower-class in England where every hint of emotion, even the socially sanctioned ones, was treated with great suspicion by the middle classes looking down on us. Any hint of feeling is seen as a breach of decorum, a sign of indignity. To strive for my own emotional competence, for emotional honesty, has felt as rebellious as anything I've done in my life.

———

In the 1980s a couple of biologists named Robert Sapolsky and Lisa Share followed a troop of wild baboons in Kenya. They witnessed the alpha males eating regularly from a garbage dump, which they refused to allow the weaker males and females to eat from. They wanted the food all to themselves, at the expense of the rest of the troop. Over time, infected meat in the garbage pile caused the death of most of the adult males, including all the alphas who had bullied the entire pack.

Eventually, aggression all but vanished from the troop. The young males that survived were raised entirely by the females and the weaker males who were left. With less need for aggressive policing of resources, everyone spent more time grooming and taking care of one another. The culture changed overnight. The pack even developed a self-policing strategy to shun the young males that flirted with aggression. The scientists termed it "the no-asshole rule."

———

I have learned that my feelings happen constantly and often without explanation, pattern, or sense of reason. Emotions, in all their unpredictability and intensity, hold immense power over my actions and perceptions. Paying attention to our interior life is not just the work of poets and therapists. Our feelings are our lives. They are our reality. We cannot neglect them. We must recognize them, like the ornithologist notices the birds, common and rare. We must choose which ones to feed. And then watch as they all, eventually, fly away from the porch.

In *Macbeth*, Macduff grapples with profound grief upon learning of his family's brutal murder, prompting Malcolm to urge him to confront the harrowing news and "dispute it like a man." Macduff replies, "I shall do so. But I must also feel it as a man." The temptation is always to respond before we truly feel.

When obstacles come across our path, the immediate impulse is to react swiftly, to exert our will upon the world. While there are instances where such assertiveness is warranted, most everyday encounters necessitate a deeper connection with our internal emotional landscape. To understand that human existence is intrinsically woven with an intricate tapestry of feelings, requiring a heightened awareness of the nuances and depths of our emotional experiences. Our hearts demand our attention.

You might say, but isn't it *action* that changes the world? Shouldn't we be focused on doing, not feeling? And you'd be right, to a point. But if we want to create a more compassionate world, a world where empathy and kindness aren't just slogans, then we have to start with ourselves. You cannot create what you do not understand. And if you don't have compassion for yourself, how will you offer it to others? Rumi was right—"You think yourself just a drop within the ocean, but you are also the ocean in a drop."

—

The first question asked by a person in the Bible is by Cain in the book of Genesis. He asks, "Am I my brother's keeper?" Men have tended to answer this question in the negative, and that, sadly, is how the human race has fared. We have to start answering this primary question differently.

Emotional competence can no longer be optional, least of all in our leaders. It must be cultivated intentionally, in our communities and in our homes. We need our own "no-asshole rule." And then, perhaps, a single generation of emotional awakening—especially in men—may change the current course of fractured humanity.

STAYING IN SHAPE

I cannot fold again
To fit into whatever
Compartment is most
Convenient for you
To keep me in—
Not even a little
At the edges or corners
Because every crease
Hurts like a betrayal.
The life within me
Must live to its fullness
So you shall have to understand—
This is the shape that I am.

MEN ARE CONDITIONED . . .

Dry skin
Ingrown toenails
Ingrown hairs
Ignoring the aches
Disregarding the pains
Working in silence
Walking it off
Keeping it quiet
Playing it tough
Keeping the dentist away
Keeping the doctor at bay
Convinced this is some
Kind of righteous sacrifice
But for a sacrifice to work
You have to first believe that
Your life is something
Worth giving away

SPEAK FREELY

"I am sorry"

"I was wrong"

"I don't know"

"I've changed my mind"

"I need help"

These are the words
> of someone who is free

STAY STRONG

They say to "stay strong"
in the throng of disaster
so I let my body unravel
all its secrets of magic & memory
so that joy & sorrow & terror
& love bleed like watercolors
together at the edges
of their vivid hues
falling into serendipity
because to feel it all is to surrender
& not all surrender is loss
so I let everything live within me
like the galaxy I am
because I cannot imagine
anything stronger than the courage to live
like we are fully alive

NOMENCLATURE

Before you set your goals
say what it is
that you really want

say it out loud
with your full chest
and, if you can,
why you want it

name the fortunes that entice
name the feelings that arise
name the fears that lie
in waiting

name it all to ensure
that you don't live
to serve your goals
but your goals
live in service to you

I WANT YOU TO KNOW WHERE THIS ANGER COMES FROM

I want you to know where this anger comes from
because it is not born from fear or hatred

as you may have misconstrued. No, it rises
from the most tender part of me, where I love

the deepest and care the most, it is soft
like magma under the earth's crust but when

I am moved and fractured like tectonic plates
shifting, the surface gives way to a molten

indignation that is not self-righteous rage
but compassion ignited, my kindness ablaze.

SENSITIVE CONTENT

This poem may contain sensitive content
It's me.
I'm the sensitive content.

I'M STILL SINGING

I was the only boy in the school choir
fated to sing the "Once in Royal David's City" solo
I never considered doing what you love
to be rebellious. I didn't know men had to be
afraid like that.

I learned the parts
elevation in harmony
tension in countermelody

I became the tenor at church for weddings
with ruffle & melody & red face,
watching the men mumble the hymns.

I am still singing
when no one else
knows the words.

YOU ARE NOT A WARRIOR. YOU ARE A BEGINNER.

After Guile defeats Ken
       in Street Fighter 2
he tells the vanquished
       "Go home and be a family man."
Doesn't he know
       that is the hardest fight of all?

I AM NOT YOUR CUP OF TEA

I am not your cup of tea
because I am made too strong
and frankly, too hot
for you to enjoy
maybe you can tolerate me
in tiny sips but I don't want
to be tolerated. I want to be
devoured by those who value
all I am and who do not wish
I was in any way watered down
to meet your tepid tastes.

LIKE MARROW

There are some sorrows
that become a part of you
like marrow
they run through your bones
so you no longer speak
of "healing" them
because that would leave you
lifeless
so they age with you
grow with you
recede with you
and in that way
they too shall pass
with you
back to the dust

AUTOBOTS & DECEPTICONS

All pain is transformed
either into meaning
as beauty & growth
or as malignance aimed
towards other people

You may not be responsible
for the source of your pain
but you are responsible
for everywhere it goes

FLOWER POWER

What a world it is that insists
a man, such as I am, can never
appreciate a marigold
as if to love a flower
is a frailty to be cured
a queerness to be ridiculed
a sign that "real men"
are not long for this age
and the world without
a retrograde masculinity
will collapse into oblivion

But if I can tear down a patriarchy
just by holding a flower
then that is the power of God
made perfect in weakness.

I CANNOT PLAY IT COOL

I cannot play it cool
 while the world is on fire
I play it earnest
I play it heart-on-sleeve
 and that heart is bleeding
I play it speak-what-you-want
I play it say-what-you-mean
I play it aching & hungry
I play it con affetto
I leave the affected coolness
 to the rigid & afraid

I AM A PROMISE I HAVE TO KEEP

The most consistent lie
I tell myself
is that next week
won't be as busy
but it's guaranteed
to be that way
if I keep saying "yes"
to everyone but me

SOME NIGHTS I DON'T RETURN

Some nights I don't return
to myself. Though I always try
to make it back. The stage door is
ajar. They say, life is a journey
but I know it as comings & goings.

A dog chases its own tail
but only bites it once. Yet
round & round it goes.
Is it instinct or stupidity
or hope? And what is the difference?

If you stand still
the buried things rise
like a million worms demanding attention
in intricate patterns

And even if I make it back to myself
the amber glow of nostalgia
colors perception
clouding the present
obscuring the door

It makes sense to call this
a crisis, but it is actually
a choice:
dance with my shadow
or sink into my bones?

A REAL SHOCK

The real shock
is not finding out
what people really think
      of you
but in finding out
how seldom they do—
        you are more free
        than you realize.

FELT CUTE

Felt cute
will probably delete later
not because I will be
any less cute
but because I will feel
un-cute
and feelings
are much harder to delete
than pictures

ACCOMMODATION

I'm fine

you choose

no worries

if not

don't mind

either way

whatever

whenever

wherever is

most convenient

for you

pretend I am

not even here

A THOUSAND LITTLE DEATHS

And when you wake from the thousandth little death:

What awaits you? Eternal rest? A new body? Valhalla?

No, just the prospect of dying a thousand times more.

So why do we keep going?

Because learning how to die well

is how you learn to live.

BITTERSWEET

Being grateful
is not an antidote
to feeling sad
but like a dollop of honey
into burnt coffee
it helps with the bitterness

THE GOLDFINCH

Under the knotted oak in the garden
I would place things to be found
or returned to, in some imagined future.

I filled an old Roses tin with trinkets & toys.
I clawed deep to pile the loamless clay
upon the metal coffin.

Later, I dug
an adjacent plot to plant the body
of a fledgling goldfinch.

I found it fallen from a nest
a carcass in the grass
a thousand songs that never were.

In my dreams, I am always younger,
never older.
Everything we bury, we bury at our roots.

NINE

HAUNTED & EXHAUSTED

The worst church experience I've ever had was also the most curated. It was at a megachurch in Southern California on a Saturday afternoon, the first of the seven weekend services. I doubt that there was a single difference in the subsequent six repetitions. The campus was set out like a theme park sprawl. Fifty percent parking lot. We were greeted by a company of professional welcomers who carried the charm and aura of car salesmen.

After the choreographed music and invocations to give money, a famous fella from Colorado Springs delivered a sermon about addiction. The climax of the talk was the revelation of his own personal struggle with an addictive substance: coffee. That's the confession of a sexual deviant if ever I've heard one. As an encore, you could get baptized, if that's the vibe you were feeling.

I am exhausted by hollow experiences in religious institutions; turned off by both megachurch phoniness and the new-age influencer grift. I am tired of pastors who dine with megadonors and not the dying. I am exhausted by churches where love is a sermon preached to ten thousand amens—all while queer folk are told they can never fall into the magic of love themselves.

Yet, I am haunted by how grateful I am for all this life and how that gratitude demands for me to send it somewhere. The best address I have to send the gratitude to is what I can only name as God.

I am exhausted by endless dry-mouth theologizing instead of a living faith. I'm not interested in tearing everything down for the sake of catharsis or philosophical superiority, but all the pedestals need toppling, even the one I sit on now. I crave a faith that breathes, that moves, that serves—something real, not simply analyzed and criticized to the point of sterilization. Deconstruction is often more of the same. It is helpful to the extent it breaks down everything that hinders us from being more compassionate. Beyond that? I am a skeptic.

I am haunted by the man from Galilee who was friends with sex workers and spent his life in conflict with political & religious leaders. A man who tells me to let the dead bury the dead. Who tells me his sufferings are my sufferings. And that mine are his. A man who reassures me that my feet deserve to be washed and that I should wash the feet of others. A man who knows the only way to find life is to fully embrace the inevitability of death.

I am exhausted by all the work I have to do just to translate spiritual jargon to decipher who is genuine, who is deluded, and who is a shyster. I am tired of "fauxnerability" and the weaponizing of therapy-speak to coddle narcissists. I am exhausted by mission funds, vision Sundays, and the tithing grift. I am so tired of vampiric faith hustles of all persuasions. I am so tired of persuasion.

Yet, I am haunted by a Holy Ghost who gets a kick out of telling me "Yep, this is all wrong." Who tells me not to abandon every spiritual practice, especially if I intend to resist. That I shouldn't neglect to pray and fast and feast and sing and meditate and ruminate and confess. To bless the food I'm grateful for and read the verses that steel my soul. All of that can help me now because it has helped me before. Not because it is my duty or burden or the law, but because these things are wells that have already been dug. They hold water that has sated prophets, saints, heroines, & sages for centuries or more. Solitude is essential for the health of a soul, but the cure for institutional failure is not isolation.

All spiritual rebellion is an entirely communal maneuver. It is connected to the ancestors who preceded us and the generations to come. We reflect, yes, but we also gather. We show up for each other in churches, in mosques, in living rooms, around kitchen tables. We listen to each other's stories, not as passive spectators, but as active participants in a shared struggle to understand, to transcend.

The myth in modern life is that we can find meaning on our own. That somehow, with enough books, enough meditation, enough self-discipline, we will unlock the mysteries of our existence, all from the safety of our own solitude. However, the divine—whatever name we give it—speaks most clearly in the spaces where our lives intersect, where we catch glimpses of ourselves in the lives of others. Healthy spirituality demands that we engage with the messy, imperfect, uncomfortable work of community. We must risk vulnerability, and disappointment. Lest the only voice of God we ever hear is the one inside our head.

A LIST OF SPIRITUAL DISCIPLINES TO PRACTICE

Active contentment
Passive ambition
Generosity until it hurts
Reading something
    people have feasted on for millennia
Writing something
    only you can write
Minding your own business
Sharing your story
Keeping your promises
Fasting from a luxury
Feasting after the harvest
Breathing until your heart slows
Listening until you hear the truth

LOVE THE ONE IN FRONT OF YOU

Love the one in front of you
store clerk, waitress
delivery man
love all the people that you can
& even those you think you can't
trans barista
grumpy neighbor
tipsy MAGA aunt
learn people's names & pronouns
& presume their pain is just as real
as anything that you can feel
& when you pass a cyclist
go by wide and slow
we are all in this together
so be gentle as you go

SABBATH REST

Sabbath rest
is not slamming the brakes
until you screech to a stop
for a single day of pause
before revving up again
but setting your tempo of being
to the lapping of the waves
upon the patient shore
so the rhythm of nature
matches the rhythm of your life—
remembering that you are nature as well.

THEY/THEM
(dedicated to Nex Benedict)

If God created night & day
& dawn, of course
& dusk
& the tangerine rosepink sunset
& the deep amethyst twilight
& the infant bright of morning

then to perceive the world in binary
is to forgo knowledge of the divine.

PIPELINE

There are many
who used to say
"God told me . . ."
who now say
"My therapist told me . . ."
to justify doing
what they want to do

eventually you must dare
to fix your own name
to your desires

INERRANCY

I keep the canon of Psalms incomplete
to accept a creative chaos that cannot
be brought into proper order. Godsong
springs surprise in the most familiar settings.
If I can see the magenta spirals bursting forth
from the dogwood branches, then all is not certain
& if bubblegum-colored corolla complements, nay
contrasts, the blue steel of Carolina sky,
then completion is still a ways away,
enough to ponder it, at least. Under what authority
can you say such things? It is the higher power,
the highest power, found in fallen petals, and dirt.

A LITTLE FAITH

My faith is a tempest:
unyielding, devout
sultry, nuanced
achingly beautiful
skeptical, unsure
downtrodden
outright rebellious
broke when faithful
godless when flush
ephemeral
a wedding
Flannery O'Connor
Stevie Wonder,
Rothko, Sufjan
Ocean Vuong

a faith
thrice denied
twice alive
though I might be
underselling it to you
just a little.

FUCK YOUR STARRY SKY

Fuck your starry sky
   my friend just died
Pin pricks of light
Are not going to cut it
I need you to slice the sky open

And where is the moon tonight?
And why, when it has gone,
Do we call it new?
Is it the invisible phase?

Right now, I would swap
All the transcendent wonder
I have ever known
To touch with trembling hand
Your scar, born from spear

I FEAR GOD

I fear God
in the way I fear beauty
in the way I fear vulnerability
in the way I fear getting what I want
in the way I fear being helpless
in the way I fear
                being loved
                        unconditionally

WHAT HOBBY LOBBY WON'T TELL YOU

Live, Laugh, Love
But also
Die, Cry, Hate.
Everything in its season.

DEFAULT LINES

My religion,
my nationality,
my culture,
my traditions,
my experience,
my feelings,
my perspective,
are not the default settings for truth.
The fruit of humility
is abundant curiosity.

VINEGAR

I am convinced
there is nothing more hopeless
than constant positivity—
the sheer tyranny of it.
I would rather
sleep in the darkness
& eat the fruit of sadness,
taste the bitter wine
& make grief a brother,
& take up my cross
& then, in waiting, discover
how death can lose its sting.

WATER INTO WINE

I went to church
It was the same old shit
Just a pastor on a stage
Spittin' from his pulpit
A man with a *vision*
Unveiling his plan
To empty your pockets
Give 'em all that you can

Couldn't take another
Minute of talk
So I took out my flask
And started to walk
A woman cried out
"He's got a demon!"
I said "Too right, sister
I think I've got three of 'em"

Went to the prayer house
To meet with God
But they were talking abortions
And rivers of blood
Getting all het up
About the future of Israel
While the bullets rain down
On the "children of Ishmael"

Striding the streets
In the city of Kansas
I was stopped by a man
Who was hungry and homeless

He said "Brother
Could you bum me a smoke?"
I said "Here, take the packet
And light one for Jesus"

PROFANITY PRAYER

Sometimes I cuss when I pray
And if you don't approve
You can go suck a benediction

GREATER LOVE HAS NO MAN

Greater love has no man
Than would lay down his life
For his three preppy kids
And Proverbs 31 wife
Firmly ensconced
In a complementarian marriage
A Craftsman home
With a two-car garage*

One spot for the pickup
A second berth for the van
Putting all our savings
In a retirement plan
We're just being good Christians
We're just being good people
Trying to thread our lives
Through the eye of a needle

* In my London accent "garage" rhymes with "marriage" and this is my book so you are
the one that has to adjust. Selah.

WATERMELON

Love does not colonize
Joy does not colonize
Peace does not colonize
Patience does not colonize
Kindness does not colonize
Goodness does not colonize
Faithfulness does not colonize
Gentleness does not colonize
Self-control does not colonize

WHITE JESUS MUST DIE

If the real Jesus
had to die
a horrific death
then you sure as hell
can slaughter
the hay-haired blond
blue eyed
pale skinned
fabrication of a savior
you have floating around
in your heart & imagination
kill that man dead
no comebacks

GENESIS

Nobody is ashamed
of themselves
until someone tells you
you should be
I know we cannot
free ourselves
so easily
but I can vow:
no one else
will learn shame from me

THIS WOULD BE MY PLEASURE

For Eve, the fruit
was not an apple
& pleasure was not the sin
God only noticed
once she wore her shame
across her gleaming skin

There is no such thing as a guilty pleasure
Because pleasure cannot assume that posture

This world is strewn
            with cruelties
So I won't hesitate
            in delight
I shall reap my joy
            from wherever it grows

OF A RAINBOW

To marvel at
the vibrant arc
of a rainbow
doesn't diminish
the devastation of a flood
it is simply a sign
we made it through

THAT OLD FAMILIAR CAGE
(OR I WON'T GO BACK TO EGYPT)

I will not be returning
to that old familiar cage
though it tempts me
when I am cold & lonesome

I will not be explaining
how I have become
more alive than you ever knew me
or imagined
I could possibly be

I will not justify
every decision of progress
& change. Yes, I grew
because that is what living things do.

I STILL BELIEVE IN MIRACLES

I still believe in miracles
Even though my friends
Are dying of diseases you could
Ostensibly heal if you listened
To any of my god-damn prayers
Perhaps I don't have enough
Faith to move the mountain
But if it only takes a mustard seed
All I know is, I have at least that much
As my heart is breaking twice;
First, for the loved ones who
Are slipping from my life
Like a stream I cannot hold
And secondly because
I still fucking believe.

GOD IS NOT IN CONTROL

Despite what they told you
    God is not in control

But she is
    Holding all things together

As mothers tend to do.

TEN

GIVE US BACK OUR LIVES

i.

Give us back our lives
because this is not our inheritance

this is furta sacra—
theft of the sacred

ii.

Our lives are being siphoned of goodness
and refilled with plastic & sugar & debt

we are operating on calorie deficits
and intrusive thoughts

we make our hunger
everybody else's problem

most of us spinning in jobs we hate
the only promise:

promotion to middle-manager
of people stuck in jobs they hate

thinking about the lunch break
from the minute we arrive

thinking about the weekend
thinking about vacation

learn to code
they say

for pizza parties, headaches
& sensory overload

for a coffee
twice reheated

for indigestion from fast food
we ate too quick

for vitamin supplements
& coping mechanisms

we secretly wish to get sick
just to get a few days rest

(nothing too serious)

we dream about winning the lottery
but never buy a ticket

(too smart for that)

we unsubscribe from email lists
like it's our job

(it isn't)

we rewatch *The Office* on one screen
fill the Amazon cart with the other

we have two dozen open tabs

we make free content for tech companies
and then they show *us* ads

we lift weights & dumbbells
& pay monthly for the privilege

we eat flavorless tomatoes
in February

the only drugs they will prescribe
are the ones you can't enjoy

there's a low-level anger
wound up like a coil

AI anxieties
kept on a rolling boil

my watch tells me to "breathe"
I tell it to fuck off

I walk into rooms
& forget why I entered

there is nothing here
I remember wanting

the cities of our fathers
are all gerrymandered & gentrified

we can't even see the shooting stars
that pass, fast & bright, above us

it wasn't the working class
who ravaged the bourgeoisie

it was the avarice
of the ultra-rich

who picked the cotton in my tee?
it's the same old shit

they just moved the plantations
out of sight, out of regulation

this system makes us all thieves
& I will never be this innocent again

they take away our recycling
but we have our suspicions

we used to watch TV together
now we sit in different rooms
each of us left
to our own devices

we become what we tolerate

I keep a tally of everything
my kids will tell their therapist about
and then I tweet about self-care
there are no maps anymore
    only phones
there are no mentors anymore
    only youtube instructional videos
even my bible
    is just another app

I drink water all day
yet wake up thirsty every night
the subcutaneous fat
in my neck thrumming
like an apartment radiator
where the thermostat is busted
or set too high

neither side of the pillow is cool enough

iii.

I am coping, but not coping
I count my teeth with my tongue

I scramble to hold on to something, anything
that doesn't move

all this creative energy with nowhere to go
eats us from within

the sadness never leaves
but neither does the wonder
& that makes everything sadder

it's all too much
    but also
nowhere near enough

iv.

It's not the pain that worries me
    it's succumbing to the numbness

I have tried a disaffected zen-state of being—
    to Lebowski my way through this world

but you can't
    the Nihilism always catches up to you

you have to care
    you have to fucking care

I am incompatible with the status quo
I will be an agent of another way of living

I am taking the American dream
and making it my footstool

we are inside the empire
& I want to fight these bastards for real

work from home if you can
because they hate it

grow anything you are able to
nurture every creature you meet

yes, everyone is struggling right now
so please be gracious

be kind & patient, but subvert
every institution that relies on our suffering

(even the churches)

we do not balk from work
there is no shortage of endeavor
in the spirit of folk

we will not be severed
from planet, personhood or kin
for nothing more
than money

v.

I cherish the mornings
when I am awoken by the birds
not by alarm
I love the days that cannot be seized
when the coffee is for leisure

or the pleasure of taste
rather than to jolt my brain
into function

time is the only commodity I care about

time to heal & dream
& pick the flowers
& feel the breeze
& be baptized in nature
& play catch with my child
& fetch with my dog
& paint
& spin a pot
& write a book
    that bigots want to ban
& bake bread
& make love
& laugh until it hurts

& miss what is lost
& remember all
    that should not be forgotten
& forget everything
    that doesn't matter
& forgive all
    that can be released

we let go of everything, eventually.

I want to receive
    this precious life
by sleeping
    when I am tired
by eating
    when I am hungry

by resting
    when I am in pain
there is no virtue in
    the denial of necessity
& having what we need
    should not be a fantasy

we hear the murmurs
from the marrow of the earth

we have the memory of real life in our bones—
the old ways are in our blood

but don't get sentimental
get free

it's okay to live a life
that people don't understand

not every horse can be broken
not all wildness can be tamed

there's a reason it's called
unbridled joy

touch grass
touch trees
touch the petals
touch the leaves
touch the water in the creek

sense this world in scent
through sight, in texture

vi.

the world is a cathedral
& my heart is a gospel choir

I can hear it
I can hear it
the year of Jubilee

and we will sing our love
while the world ain't fair

& like the first buds of spring—
I can't wait to see you bloom

so if we are a generation
kissed with apocalypse

and if these really are the end times
then let us finish with a flourish, yes
flourish, dear ones, flourish.

Poetry is not only dream and vision; it is the skeleton architecture of our lives. It lays the foundations for a future of change, a bridge across our fears of what has never been before.

—AUDRE LORDE

ACKNOWLEDGMENTS

For this book, I had a village.

Nothing I have done would be possible without my partner, co-parent, co-owner, chief goat herder, and epitome of care, dearest Emilie. Love is an observable phenomenon.

To the team that brought these words onto pages and into hands: Derek, Leita, and Jessalyn at Convergent and Amy Hughes, my agent and safe shore.

To Malcolm, who kept telling me I had something when all my dreams were somewhere in the dust, and all the Common Hymnal family.

To the real ones—Chris & Audra, Ellynne & Jonathan, Cameron & Sarah, Kate, Mike & Becky, Kel & Luke, Andrew & Elizabeth, Matthew & Micah, Noah & Sarah, Mac, Sam, Nicky B, Rebecca, Ed & Liz, Tim, Jonesy, John Peters & Jennifer Lapidus.

DAVID GATE grew up in London before making his way to Belfast, Northern Ireland, and Jacksonville, Florida. He now lives in the ancient Appalachian Mountains of Asheville, North Carolina, where he writes, mills flour, and tends to a one-acre homestead with his partner and children.

Instagram: @davidgatepoet